# The Essence of Socrates

# The Essence of Socrates

### Edited with an Introduction by
## Hunter Lewis

*The Essence of*... series of books are edited versions of great works of moral philosophy, distilled to reveal the essence of their authors' thought and argument. To read the complete, unedited version of this work, and see the excised passages, please visit our website at www.AxiosPress.com.

Axios Press
PO Box 457
Edinburg, VA 22824
888.542.9467    info@axiosinstitute.org

**Library of Congress Cataloging-in-Publication Data**

Names: Lewis, Hunter, editor.
Title: The essence of Socrates / edited with an introduction by Hunter Lewis.
Description: Edinburg : Axios Press, 2017. | Series: The essence of-- series | Includes bibliographical references and index.
Identifiers: LCCN 2016054507 (print) | LCCN 2017000796 (ebook) | ISBN 9781604191103 (pbk. : alk. paper) | ISBN 9781604191110 (ebook)
Subjects: LCSH: Socrates. | Plato.
Classification: LCC B317 .E89 2017 (print) | LCC B317 (ebook) | DDC 183/.2--dc23
LC record available at https://lccn.loc.gov/2016054507

# Contents

Introduction . . . . . . . . . . . . . . . . . . . . . . . . . . . . . . . . . . . . . . . . . . 1

1. Socratic Method. . . . . . . . . . . . . . . . . . . . . . . . . . . . . 13
2. The Search for Truth . . . . . . . . . . . . . . . . . . . . . . . . . 15
3. The Good. . . . . . . . . . . . . . . . . . . . . . . . . . . . . . . . . . . 17
4. The Importance of Modesty . . . . . . . . . . . . . . . . . . . 21
5. Do Not Be Judgmental. . . . . . . . . . . . . . . . . . . . . . . 23
6. The Rule of Reason . . . . . . . . . . . . . . . . . . . . . . . . . . 25
7. Avoid Sophistry . . . . . . . . . . . . . . . . . . . . . . . . . . . . . 29
8. The Value of Observation
   (When Combined with Logic) . . . . . . . . . . . . . . . . 31
9. Rein in the Emotions . . . . . . . . . . . . . . . . . . . . . . . . 33
10. The Pursuit of Wisdom . . . . . . . . . . . . . . . . . . . . . . 35
11. Ultimate Reality. . . . . . . . . . . . . . . . . . . . . . . . . . . . 41
12. An Inner Voice . . . . . . . . . . . . . . . . . . . . . . . . . . . . . 43
13. God (the Gods) . . . . . . . . . . . . . . . . . . . . . . . . . . . . 45
14. The Soul . . . . . . . . . . . . . . . . . . . . . . . . . . . . . . . . . . 47
15. Pleasure. . . . . . . . . . . . . . . . . . . . . . . . . . . . . . . . . . . 55
16. Temperance . . . . . . . . . . . . . . . . . . . . . . . . . . . . . . . 63

17. Right Conduct . . . . . . . . . . . . . . . . . . . . . . . . . . . . . 65
18. Obedience to the Law . . . . . . . . . . . . . . . . . . . . . . . 77
19. Honoring Parents . . . . . . . . . . . . . . . . . . . . . . . . . . 81
20. Marriage and Family . . . . . . . . . . . . . . . . . . . . . . . 83
21. Rights of Women . . . . . . . . . . . . . . . . . . . . . . . . . . 87
22. Friendship . . . . . . . . . . . . . . . . . . . . . . . . . . . . . . . 89
23. Training . . . . . . . . . . . . . . . . . . . . . . . . . . . . . . . . . 95
24. Care of the Body . . . . . . . . . . . . . . . . . . . . . . . . . . 101
25. Death . . . . . . . . . . . . . . . . . . . . . . . . . . . . . . . . . . 105

Bibliography . . . . . . . . . . . . . . . . . . . . . . . . . . . . . . . . . 111
Index . . . . . . . . . . . . . . . . . . . . . . . . . . . . . . . . . . . . . . 113

# Introduction

THIS BOOK MIGHT just as accurately have been titled *The Essence of Plato* rather than *The Essence of Socrates*. Our record of what Socrates is alleged to have said comes from only two principal sources: Plato's dialogues and Xenophon's *Memorabilia*. Socrates himself wrote nothing down. He spoke extemporaneously and his remarks were not recorded, so far as we can tell, on the spot, but only much later from memory.

To make matters more complicated, there is the famous Socratic Method. Socrates thought that the most important lesson he could teach was how to think. He therefore usually taught by asking questions designed to bring out the reasoning of his interlocutor. The flaw in this otherwise admirable approach was that we often never learn, or cannot be sure we have discerned, Socrates's own views.

The constant process of questioning and uncovering logical lapses would also no doubt have been annoying to some of Socrates's more self-satisfied contemporaries. If so, it might have contributed to the charges against him, that he was undermining the official religion among youth, which led to his condemnation and death. In *The Apology*, Plato's account of the trial and death, Socrates candidly acknowledged that:

> I go about testing and examining every man
> whom I think wise, whether he be a citizen
> or a stranger, as God has commanded me;
> and whenever I find that he is not wise, I
> point out to him on the part of God that
> he is not wise.

This does seem to be a formula for offending powerful people.

It seems a reasonable guess that Socrates did say this, or something like it. What motive would Plato have had for fabricating such a sincere but also endearingly naïve sentiment? Socrates also makes a great many direct statements in Plato's later dialogue, *The Republic*, unlike in some of the earlier dialogues specifically about him, when the Socratic Method so often veils his view. As a result, *The Republic* is often quoted in this short collection of Socrates sayings. But because it is a later dialogue, and less specifically about Socrates, it is reasonable to wonder whether the views expressed are truly those of Socrates, or rather Plato's much later interpretation or even modification of them. Unfortunately there is no way to know. Like the Gospel accounts of Jesus's sayings, which were written down long after his death, they are all we have of Socrates, and we must take them as we find them.

The combined wisdom of Socrates (469–399 BCE) and Plato (428–347 BCE) comes to us from a very long time ago. In the context of their time, they are startlingly original. There is nothing like them except, to a degree, in the contemporaneous and very advanced civilization of India. It is not surprising that they have had such an immense influence on human thought.

It is also something of a miracle that we have them at all. Plato is believed to have written philosophical treatises that he considered his main life's work. But they are all gone. What remains is the dialogues, which may have been meant for the general educated public rather than other philosophers and are therefore written in a more popular style.

*The Essence of Socrates* is very short and can be read at one sitting. Here are a few sayings of Socrates to whet the reader's appetite.

## The Central Role of Logic:

> Whenever a person strives, by the help of logic
> and dialectics, to start in pursuit of reality
> by a simple process of reason, independent

of all sensory information—never flinching, until by an act of the pure intelligence, he has grasped the real nature of good—he arrives at the very end of the intellectual journey.... Unless he does ... this, ... he dreams and sleeps away his ... life.

Plato, *The Republic*

## The Nature of Dialectic:

Is it the case that everything, which has an opposite, is generated only out of its opposite? ... In fact, is it not a universal law, even though we do not always express it in so many words, that opposites are generated always out of one another, and that there is a process of generation out of one into the other?

Plato, *Phædo*

Evils, Theodorus, can never perish; for there must always remain something which is opposite to good.

Plato, *Theætetus*

## Logic, Not Sense Experience, Is the Teacher:

And will not a man attain to this pure thought most completely, if he goes to each thing, as far as he can, with his mind alone, taking neither sight nor any other sense along with his reason in the process of thought, to be an encumbrance?

Plato, *Phædo*

## The Universe Is Itself Governed by Logic:

Shall we say that the power of an irrational principle governs all things, and that, which is called the universe, at random, and as may happen? Or, on the contrary,... that Mind, and a certain wonderful Intellect, arranges things together, and governs throughout?

Plato, *Philebus*

## The Fatal Lure of Vanity:

If I were to claim to be at all wiser than others, it would be because I do not think that I have any clear knowledge about the world, when, in fact, I have none.

Plato, *The Apology*

## What Is Truly Valuable:

Athenians, I hold you in the highest regard and love; but I will obey God rather than you; and as long as I have breath and strength, I will not cease from philosophy

and from exhorting you, and declaring:
are you not ashamed of caring so much
for the making of money, and for reputation, and for honor? Will you not think
or care about wisdom, and truth, and the
perfection of your soul?

Plato, *The Apology*

## The Soul, Not the Body:

The soul is most like the divine, the immortal, the intelligible, the uniform, the
indissoluble and the unchangeable; while
the body is most like the human, the mortal, the unintelligible, the multiform, the
dissoluble, and the changeable.

Plato, *Phædo*

It seems that there is a narrow path which
will bring us safely to our journey's end, with
reason as our guide. As long as we have this
body, and an evil of that sort is mingled with
our souls, we shall never fully gain what we
desire, which is truth. For the body is forever taking up our time with the care which
it needs; and, besides whenever diseases
attack it, they hinder us in our pursuit of
real being. It fills us with passions, desires

and fears, and all manner of phantoms, and much foolishness; and so, as the saying goes, in very truth we can never think at all for it.... While we live, we shall come nearest to knowledge, if we have no communion or intercourse with the body beyond what is absolutely necessary, and if we are not defiled with its nature. We must live pure from it until God himself releases us.

Plato, *Phædo*

## But Neither Is the Body to Be Neglected or Shown Disrespect:

He earnestly recommended those who conversed with him to take care of their health, both by learning whatever they could respecting it from men of experience, and by attending to it, each for himself, throughout his whole life, studying what food or drink, or what exercise, was most suitable for him, and how he might act in regard to them so as to enjoy the best health; for he said it would be difficult for a person who thus attended to himself to find a physician that would tell better than himself what was conducive to his health.

Xenophon, *The Memorabilia of Socrates*

## We Should Try to Free Ourselves from Desire:

You, who do not even wait for the natural desire of gratification, but fill yourself with all manner of dainties before you have an appetite for them, eating before you are hungry, drinking before you are thirsty, procuring cooks that you may eat with pleasure, buying costly wines that you may drink with pleasure, and running about seeking for snow in summer, while, in order to sleep with pleasure, you prepare not only soft beds, but couches, and rockers under your couches, for you do not desire sleep in consequence of labor, but in consequence of having nothing to do; you force the sensual inclinations before they require gratification, using every species of contrivance for the purpose, and abusing male and female, for thus it is that you treat your friends, insulting their modesty at night, and making them sleep away the most useful part of their day.

Xenophon, *The Memorabilia of Socrates*

He was not only superior to all corporeal pleasures, but also to those attendant on the acquisition of money.

Xenophon, *The Memorabilia of Socrates*

So frugal was he, that I do not know whether anyone could not earn . . . sufficient to have satisfied Socrates.

Xenophon, *The Memorabilia of Socrates*

Do you think that a philosopher will care very much about what are called pleasures, such as the pleasures of eating and drinking? . . . Or about the pleasures of sexual passion?

Plato, *Phædo*

The soul of a philosopher will consider that it is the office of philosophy to set her free. . . . She gains for herself peace from worldly things, and follows reason and ever abides in it, contemplating what is true and divine and real, and fostered by them.

Plato, *Phædo*

## But Pleasure Too Should Not Be Despised:

Another person saying that he ate without pleasure, "Acumenus," said Socrates, "prescribes an excellent remedy for that disease." The other asking, "What sort of remedy?" "To abstain from eating," said Socrates; "for he says that, after abstaining, you will live with more pleasure, less expense, and better health."

Xenophon, *The Memorabilia of Socrates*

## We Should Try to Free Ourselves from Vengeance:

We ought not to repay wrong with wrong or do harm to any man, no matter what we may have suffered from him.

Plato, *Crito*

## And We Should Not Fear Death:

To fear death, my friends, is only to think ourselves wise, without being wise; for it is to think that we know what we do not know. For everything that men can tell, death may be the greatest good that can happen to them; but they fear it as if they knew quite well that it was the greatest of evils. And what is this but that shameful ignorance of thinking that we know what we do not know?

Plato, *The Apology*

He who is truly a man, ought not to care about living a certain time; . . . he leaves all that to God and considers in what way he can spend his appointed term.

Plato, *Gorgias*

Do you think that a spirit full of lofty thoughts, and privileged to contemplate

all time, and all existence, can possibly attach any great importance to this life? "No,
it is impossible." Then such a person will not
regard death as a formidable thing, will he?

Plato, *The Republic*

—Hunter Lewis

# 1

# Socratic Method

B UT, MY FRIENDS, I believe that only God is really wise, and that . . . men's wisdom is worth little or nothing. I do not think that he meant that Socrates was wise. He only made use of my name, and took me as an example, as though He would say to men, "He among you is the wisest, who, like Socrates, knows that in very truth his wisdom is worth nothing at all." And therefore I go about testing and examining every man whom I think wise, whether he be a citizen or a stranger, as God has commanded me; and whenever I find that he is not wise, I point out to him on the part of God that he is not wise. And I am so busy in this pursuit that I have never had leisure to take any part worth mentioning in public matters, nor to look after my private affairs. I am in very great poverty by reason of my service to God.

Plato, *The Apology*

When my sons grow up, . . . my friends, . . . vex them in the same way that I have vexed you, if they seem to you to care for riches, or for any other thing, before virtue; and, if they think that they are something when they are nothing at all, reproach them, as I have reproached you, for not caring for what they should and for thinking that they are great men, when in fact they are worthless.

Plato, *The Apology*

## 2

# The Search for Truth

THE GENUINE LOVER of knowledge must, from his youth up, strive intensely after all truth.

Plato, *The Republic*

I am not a clever speaker in any way at all; unless, indeed, by a clever speaker they mean a man who speaks the truth.

Plato, *The Apology*

And you, if you take my advice, will think, not of Socrates, but of the truth; and you will agree with me, if you think that what I say is true, otherwise you will oppose me with every argument that you have.

Plato, *Phædo*

# 3

# The Good

THOUGH KNOWLEDGE AND truth are both very beautiful things, you will be right in looking upon good as something distinct from them, and even more beautiful.

Plato, *The Republic*

None will know the just and the beautiful satisfactorily till he knows the good.

Plato, *The Republic*

The essential form of the good is the highest object of thought, and that . . . essence, by blending with just things and all other created objects, renders them useful and advantageous. . . . If, I say, we know everything else perfectly, without knowing this, it will profit us nothing; just as it would be equally profitless to possess everything without possessing what is good.

Plato, *The Republic*

Whenever a person strives, by the help of logic and dialectics, to start in pursuit of reality by a simple process of reason, independent of all sensory information—never flinching, until by an act of the pure intelligence, he has grasped the real nature of good— he arrives at the very end of the intellectual journey.

Plato, *The Republic*

Unless a person can strictly define by a process of thought the essential form of the good, abstracted from everything else, and unless he can fight his way as it were through all objections, studying to disprove them not by the rules of opinion, but by those of real existence, and unless in all these conflicts he travels to his conclusion without making one false step in his train of thought—unless he does all this, . . . he knows neither the essence of good, nor any other good thing, and . . . any phantom of it, which he may chance to apprehend, is the fruit of opinion and not of thought, and . . . he dreams and sleeps away his present life, and never wakes on this side of that future world, in which he is doomed to sleep forever?

Plato, *The Republic*

In the world of knowledge, the essential form of good is the limit of our inquiries, and can barely be perceived; but, when perceived, we cannot help concluding that it is in every case the source of all that is bright and beautiful—in the visible world giving birth to light, and its master, and in the intellectual world dispensing, immediately and with full authority, truth and reason—and that whosoever would act wisely, either in private or in public, must set this form of good before his eyes.

Plato, *The Republic*

Philebus . . . asserts, that the good is to all animals joy, pleasure and delight, and whatever else harmonizes with such kind of things; but what I contend is, that it is not those things, but that to be wise, and to understand, and to remember, and whatever is of a kindred nature, both correct opinion, and true reasonings, are better and more acceptable than pleasure, to all who are able to partake in them.

Plato, *Philebus*

The real nature of education is at variance with the account given of it by certain of its professors, who pretend, I believe, to infuse into the mind a knowledge of which it was destitute, just as sight might be instilled into blinded eyes. . . . Our present argument shows us that there is a faculty residing in the soul of each person, and an instrument enabling each of us to learn; and that, just as we might suppose it to be impossible to turn the eye round from darkness to light without turning the whole body, so must this faculty, or this instrument, be wheeled round, in company with the entire soul, from the perishing world, until it be enabled to endure the contemplation of the real world and the brightest part thereof, which, according to us, is the form of good.

Plato, *The Republic*

"But as to happiness, Socrates," said Euthydemus, "that at least appears to be an indisputable good." "Yes, Euthydemus," replied Socrates, "if we make it consist in things that are themselves indisputably good." "But what," said he, "among things constituting happiness can be a doubtful good?" "Nothing," answered Socrates, "unless we join with it beauty, or strength, or wealth, or glory, or any other such thing."

Xenophon, *The Memorabilia of Socrates*

Evils, Theodorus, can never perish; for there must always remain something which is opposite to good.

Plato, *Theætetus*

# 4

# The Importance of Modesty

I T IS . . . THE knowledge of one's self to know what one knows and what one does not know.

Plato, Charmides

I have gained this name, Athenians, simply by reason of a certain wisdom. But by what kind of wisdom? It is by just that wisdom which is, I believe, possible to men. . . . You remember Chærephon? From youth upwards he was my comrade; and he went into exile with the people and with the people he returned. And you remember, too, Chærephon's character, how vehement he was in carrying through whatever he took in hand. Once he went to Delphi and ventured to put this question to the oracle—I entreat you again, my friends, not to cry out—he asked if there was any man who was wiser than I; and the priestess answered that there was no man. Chærephon himself is dead, but his brother here will confirm what I say. . . . When I heard of the oracle I began to reflect: "What can God mean by this dark saying? I know very well that I am not wise, even in the smallest degree. Then what can He mean by saying that I am the wisest of men?" . . . So when I went away, I thought to myself, "I am wiser than this man; neither of us probably knows anything that is really good, but he thinks that he has knowledge, when he has not, while I, having no knowledge, do not think that I have. I seem, at any rate, to be a little wiser than he is on this point; I do not think that I know what I do not know."

Plato, The Apology

If I were to claim to be at all wiser than others, it would be because I do not think that I have any clear knowledge about the world, when, in fact, I have none.

Plato, The Apology

# 5

# Do Not Be Judgmental

D O YOU MEAN to say that you, who are so much younger than I, are yet so much wiser than I, that you know that bad citizens always do evil, and that good citizens always do good, to those with whom they come in contact, while I am so extraordinarily stupid as not to know.

Plato, *The Apology*

# 6

# The Rule of Reason

Do we not . . . call a man temperate, . . . when [those] governed by [passion and ambition] regard . . . the rational principle as the rightful sovereign, and set up no opposition to its authority?

Plato, *The Republic*

As those who do not exercise the body cannot perform what is proper to the body, so those who cannot exercise the mind, cannot perform what is proper to the mind; for they can neither do that which they ought to do, nor refrain from that from which they ought to refrain.

Xenophon, *The Memorabilia of Socrates*

Is it not, then, essentially the province of the rational principle to command, inasmuch as it is wise and has to exercise forethought in behalf of the entire soul, and the province of the spirited principle to be its subject and ally?

Plato, The Republic

You can touch . . . , and see . . . , and perceive . . . with the other senses, while you can grasp the unchanging only by the reasoning of the intellect.

Plato, Phædo

And will not a man attain to this pure thought most completely, if he goes to each thing, as far as he can, with his mind alone, taking neither sight nor any other sense along with his reason in the process of thought, to be an encumbrance?

Plato, Phædo

Do you conceive that those who, unaided by the pure reason, entertain a correct opinion, are at all superior to blind men, who manage to keep the straight path?

Plato, The Republic

To hate reasoning is the greatest evil that can happen to us.

Plato, Phædo

He who has his thoughts truly set on the things that really exist, cannot even spare time to look down upon the occupations of men, and, by disputing with them, catch the infection of malice and hostility. On the contrary, he devotes all his time to the contemplation of certain well-adjusted and changeless objects; and, beholding how they neither wrong, nor are wronged by, each other, but are all obedient to order and in harmony with reason, he studies to imitate and resemble them as closely as he can.

Plato, *The Republic*

Possessing neither mind, nor memory, nor thought, nor a true opinion, it is surely necessary for you, in the first place, to be ignorant, whether you had any joy, or not, being void of all intellect.

Plato, *Philebus*

# 7

# Avoid Sophistry

To use words wrongly is not only a fault in itself; it also creates evil in the soul.

Plato, *Phædo*

Whenever, then, an orator, who is ignorant of good and evil, finds a people in a state of similar ignorance, and takes upon himself to persuade them by passing an eulogium, not upon a poor ass as though it were a horse, but upon evil as though it were good; and when, by having studied and learned the popular opinions, he has succeeded in persuading them to do that which is evil instead of that which is good, what kind of fruit do you imagine his oratory will hereafter reap as the harvest of the seed he has sown?

Plato, *Phædrus*

You have noticed that, whenever boys sample dialectic for the first time, they pervert it into an amusement and ever make use of it for purposes of contradiction, and imitate in their own persons the artifices of those who study refutation—delighting, like puppies, in pulling and tearing to pieces, by means of logic, anyone who comes near them. . . . The man of more advanced years, on the contrary, will not suffer himself to be led away by such madness; but will imitate those who are resolved to discuss and examine truth, rather than those who play at controversy for amusement; and, as a consequence of his superior discretion, he will increase, instead of diminish, the general respect for the pursuit.

Plato, *The Republic*

# 8

# The Value of Observation (When Combined with Logic)

CONCERNING CELESTIAL MATTERS in general, he dissuaded every man from becoming a speculator how the divine power contrives to manage them; for he did not think that such points were discoverable by man, nor did he believe that those acted dutifully toward the gods who inquired into things which they did not wish to make known. He observed, too, that a man who was anxious about such investigations, was in danger of losing his senses, not less than Anaxagoras, who prided himself highly on explaining the plans of the gods, lost his. . . . For Anaxagoras, when he said that fire and the sun were of the same nature, did not reflect that people can easily look upon fire, but cannot turn their gaze to the sun, and that men, if exposed to the rays of the sun, have complexions of a darker shade, but not if exposed to fire; he omitted to consider, too, that of the productions of the earth, none can come fairly to maturity without the rays of the sun, while, if warmed by the heat of fire, they all perish; and when he said that the sun was a heated stone, he forgot that a stone placed in the fire does not shine, or last long, but that the sun continues perpetually the most luminous of all bodies.

Xenophon, *The Memorabilia of Socrates*

Be not ignorant of yourself, my friend, and do not commit the error which the majority of men commit; for most persons, though they are eager to look into the affairs of others, give no thought to the examination of their own. Do not you, then, neglect this duty but strive more and more to cultivate your own powers.

Xenophon, *The Memorabilia of Socrates*

# 9

# Rein in the Emotions

And now to the person who asserts that it is profitable for this creature, man, to be unrighteous, and that it is not for his interest to do justice, let us reply that his assertion amounts to this, that it is profitable for him to feast and strengthen the multifarious monster and the lion and its members, and to starve and enfeeble the man to such an extent as to leave him at the mercy of the guidance of either of the other two, without making any attempt to habituate or reconcile them to one another, but leaving them together to bite and struggle and devour each other.

Plato, *The Republic*

The mind of a man under the influence of desire always either seeks after the object of desire, or to attract to itself that which it wishes to have.

Plato, *The Republic*

When a man is overpowered by desires against the dictates of his reason, he reviles himself, and resents the violence thus exerted within him, and that, in this struggle of contending parties, the spirit sides with the reason?

Plato, *The Republic*

Those who are bewitched, you would yourself, I believe, assert to be those who change their opinion either through the seductions of pleasure or under the pressure of fear.

Plato, *The Republic*

And in the case of love and anger, and all the mental sensations of desire, grief, and pleasure, which, as we hold, accompany all our actions, is it not true that poetic imitation works upon us similar effects? For it waters and cherishes these emotions, which ought to wither with drought, and constitutes them our rulers, when they ought to be our subjects, if we wish to become better and happier instead of worse and more miserable.

Plato, *The Republic*

A good man, if he meet with a misfortune, like that of losing a son or anything else that he values most highly, will bear it more easily than anyone else.

Plato, *The Republic*

## 10

# The Pursuit of Wisdom

SOCRATES THEN SAID, "Tell me, Euthydemus, have you ever gone to Delphi? . . . And did you observe what is written somewhere on the temple wall, KNOW THYSELF? . . . And did you take no thought of that inscription, or did you attend to it, and try to examine yourself, to ascertain what sort of character you are?

"Is it not evident, . . . that men enjoy a great number of blessings in consequence of knowing themselves, and incur a great number of evils through being deceived about themselves? For they who know themselves know what is suitable for them, and distinguish between what they can do and what they cannot; and, by doing what they know how to do, procure for themselves what they need, and are prosperous, and by abstaining from what they do not know, live blamelessly, and avoid being unfortunate? By this knowledge of themselves, too, they can form an opinion of other men, and, by their experience concerning the rest of mankind, obtain for themselves what is good, and guard against what is evil.

"But they who do not know themselves, but are deceived about their own powers, are in similar case with regard to other men, and other human affairs, and neither understand what they require, nor what they are doing, nor the characters of those with whom they connect themselves; but, being in error as to all these particulars, they fail to obtain what is good, and fall into evil.

"They, on the other hand, who understand what they take in hand, succeed in what they attempt and become esteemed and honored; those who resemble them in character willingly form connections with them; those who are unsuccessful in life desire to be assisted by their advice, and to prefer them to themselves; they place in them their hopes of good, and love them, on all these accounts, beyond all other men."

Xenophon, *The Memorabilia of Socrates*

I went instead to each one of you by himself, to do him, as I say, the greatest of services, and strove to persuade him not to think of his affairs, until he had thought of himself, and tried to make himself as perfect and wise as possible.

Plato, The Apology

And if I tell you that no better thing can happen to a man than to converse every day about virtue and the other matters about which you have heard me conversing and examining myself and others, and that an unexamined life is not worth living, then you will believe me still less. But that is the truth, my friends, though it is not easy to convince you of it.

Plato, The Apology

If you were therefore to say to me, "Socrates, this time we will not listen to Anytus; we will let you go, but on this condition, that you cease from carrying on this search of yours, and from philosophy. If you are found following those pursuits again, you shall die." I say, if you offered to let me go on these terms, I should reply:

Athenians, I hold you in the highest regard and love; but I will obey God rather than you; and as long as I have breath and strength, I will not cease from philosophy and from exhorting you, and declaring the truth to every one of you whom I meet, saying, as I am wont: My excellent friend, you are a citizen of Athens, a city which is very great and very famous for wisdom and power of mind: are you not ashamed of caring so much for the making of money, and for reputation, and for honor? Will you not think or care about wisdom, and truth, and the perfection of your soul?

And if he disputes my words, and says that he does not care about these things, I shall not forthwith release him and go away: I shall question him and cross-examine him and test him: and if I think that he has not virtue, though he says that he has, I shall reproach him for setting the lower value on the most important things, and a higher value on those that are of less account. This I shall do to every one whom I meet, young or old, citizen or stranger, but more especially to the citizens, for they are more nearly akin to me. For, know well, God has commanded me to do so. And I think that no better piece of fortune has ever befallen you in Athens than my service to God. For I spend my whole life in going about and persuading you all to give your first and chiefest care to the perfection of your souls, and not, till you have done that,

to think of your bodies, or your wealth;
and telling you that virtue does not come
from wealth, but that wealth, and every
other good thing which men have, whether
in public or in private, comes from virtue.

Plato, *The Apology*

I fear that virtue is not ... to be bought in this way, by
bartering pleasure for pleasure, and pain for pain, and
fear for fear, and the greater for the less, like coins.
There is only one sterling coin for which all these things
ought to be exchanged, and that is wisdom. All that is
bought and sold for this and with this, whether courage, or temperance, or justice, is real; in one word
true virtue cannot be without wisdom, and it matters
nothing whether pleasure, and fear, and all other such
things, are present or absent. But I think that the virtue which is composed of pleasures and fears bartered
with one another, and severed from wisdom, is only a
shadow of true virtue, and that it has no freedom, nor
health, nor truth. True virtue in reality is a kind of
purifying from all these things; and temperance, justice, courage and wisdom itself are the purification.

Plato, *Phædo*

I in my life have striven as hard as I was able, and
have left nothing undone that I might become one of
them, a true philosopher. Whether I have striven in

the right way, and whether I have succeeded or not, I suppose that I shall learn in a little while when I reach the other world, if it be the will of God.

Plato, *Phædo*

Observe that in the pleasure of all except the wise man, there is something positively unreal and un-genuine.

Plato, *The Republic*

For himself, he would hold discourse, from time to time, on what concerned mankind, considering what was pious, what impious; what was becoming, what unbecoming; what was just, what unjust; what was sanity, what insanity; what was fortitude, what cowardice; what a state was, and what the character of a statesman; what was the nature of government over men, and the qualities of one skilled in governing them; and touching on other subjects, with which he thought that those who were acquainted were men of worth and repute, but that those who were ignorant of them might justly be deemed no better than slaves.

Xenophon, *The Memorabilia of Socrates*

Nature . . . has implanted a love of wisdom in the mind of man.

Plato, *Phædrus*

# 11

# Ultimate Reality

LET US NOT be at all surprised at finding that things as substantial as a bed are shadowy objects when contrasted with reality.

Plato, *The Republic*

"Shall we not affirm that the body with us possesses soul?" "It is evident; we shall affirm it." "From whence, friend Protarchus, did it obtain it, unless the body of the universe happens to be with a soul and possessing the same things as this, but in every way more beautiful?"

Plato, *Philebus*

Shall we say that the power of an irrational principle governs all things, and that, which is called the universe, at random, and as may happen? Or, on the contrary, . . . that Mind, and a certain wonderful Intellect, arranges things together, and governs throughout?

Plato, *Philebus*

Tell me, Euthydemus, has it ever occurred to you to consider how carefully the gods have provided for men everything that they require?

Xenophon, *The Memorabilia of Socrates*

## 12

# An Inner Voice

I HAVE A CERTAIN divine sign from God, which is the divinity that Miletus has caricatured in his indictment. I have had it from childhood; it is a kind of voice, which, whenever I hear it, always turns me back from something which I was going to do, but never urges me to act.

Plato, *The Apology*

Know well, my dear friend Crito, that this is what I seem to hear, as the worshippers of Cybele seem, in their frenzy, to hear the music of flutes; and the sound of these words rings loudly in my ears, and drowns all other words.

Plato, *Crito*

# 13

# God (the Gods)

THE SOUL OF man, moreover, which partakes of the divine nature if anything else in man does, rules, it is evident, within us, but is itself unseen. Meditating on these facts, therefore, it behooves you not to despise the unseen gods, but, estimating their power from what is done by them, to reverence what is divine.

Xenophon, *The Memorabilia of Socrates*

To the gods he simply prayed that they would give him good things, as believing that the gods knew best what things are good.

Xenophon, *The Memorabilia of Socrates*

For he thought that the gods paid regard to men, not in the way in which some people suppose, who imagine that the gods know some things and do not know others, but he considered that the gods know all things, both what is said, what is done, and what is meditated in silence, and are present everywhere, and give admonitions to men concerning everything human.

Xenophon, *The Memorabilia of Socrates*

By delivering such sentiments, Socrates seems to me to have led his associates to refrain from what was impious, or unjust, or dishonorable, not merely when they were seen by men, but when they were in the solitude, since they would conceive that nothing that they did would escape the knowledge of the gods.

Xenophon, *The Memorabilia of Socrates*

God is good in reality, and is to be so represented.

Plato, *The Republic*

In God is no unrighteousness at all. He is altogether righteous and there is nothing more like Him than he of us who is the most righteous.

Plato, *Theætetus*

# 14

# The Soul

SPEAKING UNIVERSALLY, DOES not the cultivation of the body in all its branches contain truth and real existence in a less degree than the cultivation of the soul in all its branches? ... And do you not regard the body itself as less true and real than the soul?

Plato, *The Republic*

For all things proceed from the soul, both the good and bad, to the body and to the whole man, and flow from thence, as from the head to the eyes.

Plato, *Charmides*

Surely, then, to him who has an eye to see, there can be no fairer spectacle than that of a man who combines the possession of moral beauty in his soul with outward beauty of form, corresponding and harmonizing with the former, because the same great pattern enters into both.

Plato, *The Republic*

Grant me to be beautiful in the inner man, and all I have of outer things to be at peace with those within!

Plato, *Phædrus*

He used to say, besides, that when the soul has departed, in which alone intelligence exists, men take away the body of their dearest friend, and put it out of sight, as soon as possible.

Xenophon, *The Memorabilia of Socrates*

If you had had occasion to entrust your body to anyone's care, at the risk of its becoming either healthy or depraved, frequent would have been your deliberations on the propriety of the measure; you would have summoned both friends and relatives to a consultation and taken many days to consider the matter; yet now, when your soul is concerned, your soul, which you prize far more highly than your body, and whereon your all depends for good or ill, according as it turns out healthy or depraved; when this, I say, is at stake, you communicate neither with your father, nor your brother, nor with any of us, your friends.

Plato, *Protagoras*

Do you think that it is the duty of an immortal thing to trouble itself about this insignificant interval, and not about eternity?

Plato, *The Republic*

Unless depravity of body introduces into the soul depravity of soul, let us never suppose that the soul can be destroyed by an alien evil without the presence of its own peculiar disease; . . . let us never assert that a fever, or any other disease, or fatal violence, or even the act of cutting up the entire body into the smallest possible pieces, can have any tendency to destroy the soul.

Plato, *The Republic*

Is it the case that everything, which has an opposite, is generated only out of its opposite? . . . In fact, is it not a universal law, even though we do not always express it in so many words, that opposites are generated always out of one another, and that there is a process of generation out of one into the other?

Plato, *Phædo*

The soul is most like the divine, the immortal, the intelligible, the uniform, the indissoluble and the unchangeable; while the body is most like the human, the mortal, the unintelligible, the multiform, the dissoluble, and the changeable.

Plato, *Phædo*

Does the soul yield to the passions of the body, or does she discipline them? I mean this: When the body is hot and thirsty, does not the soul drag it away and prevent it from drinking, and when it is hungry, does she not prevent it from eating? And do we not see her opposing the desires of the body in a thousand other ways?

Plato, *Phædo*

I should be wrong, Cebes and Simmias, not to grieve at death, if I did not think that I was going to live both with other gods who are good and wise, and with men who have died, and who are better than the men of this world. But you must know that I hope that I am going to live among good men, though I am not quite sure of that. But I am as sure as I can be in such matters that I am going to live with gods who are very good masters. And therefore I am not so much grieved at death. I am confident that the dead have some kind of existence, and, as has been said of old, an existence that is far better for the good than for the wicked.

Plato, *Phædo*

I will tell you what happens to a soul which is pure at her departure, and which in her life has had no intercourse that she could avoid, with the body, and so draws after her, when she dies, no taint of the body, but has shunned it, and gathered herself into herself, for such has been her constant duty—and that only means

that she has loved wisdom rightly, and has truly practiced how to die. . . . Does not the soul, then, which is
in that state, go away to the invisible that is like herself,
and to the divine, the immortal and the wise, where
she is released from error, folly, fear and fierce passions,
and all the other evils that fall to the lot of men, and is
happy, and for the rest of time lives in very truth with
the gods, as they say that the initiated do? Shall we
affirm this, Cebes?

. . . But if she be defiled and impure when she leaves
the body, from being ever with it, and serving it and
loving it, and from being besotted by it, and by its
desires and pleasures, so that she thinks nothing true,
but what is bodily, and can be touched and seen, and
eaten, and drunk, and used for men's lusts; if she has
learned to hate, and tremble at, and fly from what is
dark and invisible to the eye, and intelligible and
apprehended by philosophy—do you think that a soul
which is in that state will be pure and without alloy at
her departure?

Plato, *Phædo*

If it be true that the soul is immortal, we have to take
care of her, not merely on account of the time which
we call life, but also on account of all time. Now we
can see how terrible is the danger of neglect. For if
death had been a release from all things, it would have
been a godsend to the wicked; for when they died,

they would have been released with their souls from the body and from their own wickedness. But now we have found that the soul is immortal; and so her only refuge and salvation from evil is to become as perfect and wise as possible. For she takes nothing with her to the other world but her education and culture; and these, it is said, are of the greatest service or of the greatest injury to the dead man, at the very beginning of his journey thither.

Plato, *Phædo*

It seems that there is a narrow path which will bring us safely to our journey's end, with reason as our guide. As long as we have this body, and an evil of that sort is mingled with our souls, we shall never fully gain what we desire, which is truth. For the body is forever taking up our time with the care which it needs; and, besides whenever diseases attack it, they hinder us in our pursuit of real being. It fills us with passions, desires and fears, and all manner of phantoms, and much foolishness; and so, as the saying goes, in very truth we can never think at all for it. And therefore, for all these reasons, we have no leisure for philosophy. And last of all, if we ever are free from the body for a time, and then turn to examine some matter, it falls in our way at every step of the inquiry.... Then, it seems, after we are dead, we shall gain the wisdom which we desire, and for which we say we have a passion, but not while we are alive, as the argument shows. . . . And while we live, we shall come nearest to knowledge, if we have no communion or intercourse with the body beyond what is absolutely necessary, and if we are not defiled with its nature. We must live pure from it until God himself releases us.

Plato, *Phædo*

The souls of the . . . evil . . . are compelled to wander . . . as a punishment for the wicked lives that they have lived; and their wanderings continue until, from the desire for the corporeal that clings to them, they are again imprisoned in a body.

And, . . . they are imprisoned, probably in the bodies of animals with habits similar to the habits which were theirs in their lifetime. By this . . . I mean that men who have practiced unbridled gluttony, and wantonness, and drunkenness, probably enter the bodies of asses, and such like animals. Do you not think so? . . . And those who have chosen injustice, and tyranny, and robbery, enter the bodies of wolves, and hawks, and kites. Where else should we say that such souls go?

Plato, *Phædo*

A man of sense will not insist that these things are exactly as I have described them. But I think that he will believe that something of the kind is true of the soul and her habitations, seeing that she is shown to be immortal, and that it is worth his while to stake everything on this belief. The venture is a fair one, and he must charm his doubts with spells like these. That is why I have been prolonging fable all this time.

Plato, *Phædo*

My belief is, not that a good body will by its own excellence, make the soul good, but, on the contrary, that a good soul will by its excellence render the body as perfect as it can be.

Plato, *The Republic*

# 15

# Pleasure

IN LAMENTS AND songs of joy, and not only in dramas, but in the whole tragedy and comedy of life, and in ten thousand other cases, pains and pleasures are mingled together. . . . For apart from pain, we should never be able fully to try pleasure.

Plato, *Philebus*

How strange a thing is what men call pleasure! How wonderful is its relation to pain, which seems to be the opposite of it! They will not come to a man together, but if he pursues the one and gains it, he is almost forced to take the other also, as if they were two distinct things united at one end.

Plato, *Phædo*

It is evident that the greatest pleasures, and likewise the greatest pains, are produced in some wickedness of the soul and of the body, and not in their virtuous state. . . . Are not those pleasures the superior, which the strongest desires precede? . . . But do not both they, who are in a fever, and those afflicted with diseases of that kind, thirst more, and shiver more, and suffer more . . . in the body, and are more conversant with the want of those things, in which, being supplied, they feel a greater pleasure? . . . Shall we deny all this to be true? . . . Should not we appear to speak correctly by saying that if anyone would know what are the greatest pleasures, he must not go and look upon the healthy, but upon the sick?

Plato, Philebus

Wicked men . . . for the most part delight in false pleasures; but the good, in the true.

Plato, Philebus

Speaking roughly, most of the so-called pleasures which reach the mind come through the body, and the keenest of them belong to this species; that is to say, they are a kind of release from pain. . . . The repose felt at the times we speak of is not really, but only appears to be, pleasant, by the side of what is painful, and painful by the side of what is pleasant; and these representations will in no instance stand the test of comparison with true delight because they are only a species of enchantment.

Plato, *The Republic*

Persons unacquainted with truth, besides holding a multitude of other unsound opinions, . . . when they are carried to what is painful, they form a correct opinion of their condition, and are really in pain, yet, when they are carried from pain to the middle point between pain and pleasure, they obstinately imagine that they have arrived at fullness of pleasure—which they have never experienced?

They tell us that nothing is pleasanter than health, but that, before they were ill, they had not found out its supreme pleasantness.

Plato, *The Republic*

He was not only superior to all corporeal pleasures, but also to those attendant on the acquisition of money.

Xenophon, *The Memorabilia of Socrates*

So frugal was he, that I do not know whether anyone could not earn . . . sufficient to have satisfied Socrates.

Xenophon, *The Memorabilia of Socrates*

Do you think that a philosopher will care very much about what are called pleasures, such as the pleasures of eating and drinking? . . . Or about the pleasures of sexual passion?

Plato, *Phædo*

As to love, his counsel was to abstain rigidly from familiarity with beautiful persons; for he observed that it was not easy to be in communication with such persons and maintain continence.

Xenophon, *The Memorabilia of Socrates*

I advise you, Xenophon, whenever you see any handsome person, to flee without looking behind you.

Xenophon, *The Memorabilia of Socrates*

For himself, he was evidently so disciplined with respect to such matters, that he could more easily keep aloof from the fairest and most blooming objects than others from the most deformed and unattractive.

Xenophon, *The Memorabilia of Socrates*

When he perceived, however, that Critias was enamored of Euthydemus, and was seeking to have the enjoyment of his society, like those who abuse the persons of others for licentious purposes, he dissuaded him from his intention, by saying that it was illiberal and unbecoming a man of honor and proper feeling, to offer supplication to the object of his affections, by whom he wished to be held in high esteem, beseeching and entreating him, like a beggar, to grant a favor, especially when such favor was for no good end.

Xenophon, *The Memorabilia of Socrates*

You, who do not even wait for the natural desire of gratification, but fill yourself with all manner of dainties before you have an appetite for them, eating before you are hungry, drinking before you are thirsty, procuring cooks that you may eat with pleasure, buying costly wines that you may drink with pleasure, and running about seeking for snow in summer, while, in order to sleep with pleasure, you prepare not only soft beds, but couches, and rockers under your couches, for you do not desire sleep in consequence of labor, but in consequence of having nothing to do; you force the sensual inclinations before they require gratification, using every species of contrivance for the purpose, and abusing male and female, for thus it is that you treat your friends, insulting their modesty at night, and making them sleep away the most useful part of their day.

Xenophon, *The Memorabilia of Socrates*

Many who can be frugal in their expenses before they fall in love, are, after falling in love, unable to continue so; and, when they have exhausted their resources, they no longer abstain from means of gain from which they previously shrunk as thinking them dishonorable.

Xenophon, *The Memorabilia of Socrates*

Can you mention any pleasure that is greater and more violent than that which accompanies the indulgence of the passion of love? ... But is it not the nature of legitimate love to desire an orderly and beautiful object in a sober and harmonious temper? ... Then nothing akin to madness or licentiousness must approach legitimate love.

Plato, *The Republic*

Of all the appetites with which the gain-loving and honor-loving elements are conversant, those which follow the leading of science and reason, and along with them pursue the pleasures which wisdom directs, till they find them, will find not only the truest pleasures that they can possibly find, in consequence of their devotion to truth, but also the pleasures appropriate to them, since what is best for each is also most appropriate. .... Hence, so long as the whole soul follows the guidance of the wisdom-loving element without any dissension, each part can not only do its own proper work in all respects, or in other words, be just; but, moreover, it can enjoy its own proper pleasures, in the best and truest shape possible.

Plato, *The Republic*

There appear to me to be three objects ... and similarly three appetites, and governing principles. ... One is ... whereby a man learns, and another whereby he shows courage. The third . . . we call appetitive, on account of the violence of the appetites of hunger, thirst and sex, and all their accompaniments; and we called it peculiarly money-loving, because money is the chief agent in the gratification of such appetites.

Now are you aware that, if you choose to ask three men representing these principles, each in his turn, which of their lives is pleasantest, each will extol his own beyond the other. . . . Then whenever a dispute is raised as to the pleasures of each kind and the life itself of each class, not in reference to degrees of beauty and deformity, of morality and immorality, but in reference merely to their position in the scale of pleasure, and freedom from pain—how can we know which of the three men speaks most truly? . . . Of the three men, which is the best acquainted by experience with all the pleasures which we have mentioned? Does the lover of gain study the nature of real truth to such an extent as to be, in your opinion, acquainted with the pleasures of knowledge better than the lover of wisdom is acquainted with the pleasure of gain? . . . The lover of wisdom is far superior to the lover of gain in practical acquaintance with both these pleasures. . . . Honor waits upon them all, if each works out the objects of his pursuit, for the rich man is honored by many people, as well as the courageous and the wise; so that all are acquainted with the nature of the pleasure to be derived from the fact of being honored. But the nature of the pleasure to be found in the contemplation of truth, none can have tasted, except the lover of wisdom. Then, as far as practical acquaintance goes, the lover of wisdom is the best judge of the three.

Plato, *The Republic*

*16*

# Temperance

PRUDENCE AND TEMPERANCE Socrates did not distinguish, for he deemed that he who knew what was honorable and good, and how to practice it, and who knew what was dishonorable, and how to avoid it, was both prudent and temperate.

Xenophon, *The Memorabilia of Socrates*

He advised them to be cautious of taking anything that would stimulate them to eat when they were not hungry, and to drink when they were not thirsty; for he said that those were the things that disordered the stomach, the head, and the mind.

Xenophon, *The Memorabilia of Socrates*

"Do not . . . the intemperate," said Socrates, "endure the very worst of slavery?"

Xenophon, *The Memorabilia of Socrates*

Intemperance, by not allowing men to withstand hunger, thirst, or the desire of sensual gratification, or want of sleep . . . (until the inclinations may be most happily indulged), hinders them from having any due enjoyment in acts most necessary and most habitual; but temperance, which alone enables men to endure the privations which I have mentioned, alone enables them to find delight in the gratifications to which I have alluded.

Xenophon, *The Memorabilia of Socrates*

Is it not the duty of every man to consider that temperance is the foundation of every virtue, and to establish the observance of it in his mind before all things? For who, without it, can either learn anything good, or sufficiently practice it? Who, that is a slave to pleasure, is not in an evil condition both as to his body and his mind?

Xenophon, *The Memorabilia of Socrates*

# 17

# Right Conduct

NOT LONG SINCE it was thought discreditable and ridiculous among the Greeks, as it is now among most barbarian nations, for men to be seen naked. . . . But when experience has shown that it was better to strip than to cover up the body, and when the ridiculous effect, which this plan had to the eye, had given way before the arguments establishing its superiority, it was at the same time, as I imagine, demonstrated, that he is a fool who thinks anything ridiculous but that which is evil.

Plato, *The Republic*

May we not assert that the practices which are held to be fair and foul, are fair or foul according as they either

subjugate the brutal parts of our nature to the man—
perhaps I should rather say, to the divine part—or
make the tame part the servant and slave of the wild?

Plato, *The Republic*

And by what argument can we uphold the advantages
of disguising the commission of injustice, and escap-
ing the penalties of it? Am I not right in supposing
that the man, who thus escapes detection, grows still
more vicious than before?

Plato, *The Republic*

Can it be profitable for anyone to take gold unjustly,
since the consequence is, that, in the moment of taking the gold, he is enslaving the best part of him to
the most vile?

Plato, *The Republic*

Those, therefore, who are unacquainted with wisdom and virtue, and who spend their time in perpet-
ual banqueting and similar indulgences, are carried
down, as it appears, and back again only as far as the
midway point on the upward road; and between these
limits they roam their life long, without ever over-
stepping them so as to look up towards, or be carried
to, the true Above, and they have never been really
filled with what is real, or tasted sure and unmin-
gled pleasure; but like cattle, they are always looking

downwards, and hanging their heads to the ground, and poking them into their dining-tables, while they graze and get fat and propagate their species; and, to satiate their greedy desire for these enjoyments, they kick and butt with hoofs and horns of iron, till they kill one another under the influence of ravenous appetites; because they fill with things unreal the unreal and incontinent part of their nature.

Plato, *The Republic*

Now of this nature are beauty, wisdom, virtue and all similar qualities. By these, then the plumage of the soul is chiefly fostered and increased; by ugliness, vice and all such contraries, it is wasted and destroyed.

Plato, *Phædrus*

Neither is subjection to self aught else than ignorance, mastery over self aught else than wisdom.

Plato, *Protagoras*

We should set the highest value, not on living, but on living well.

Plato, *Crito*

When the current has set towards thought, and all its branches, a man's desires will, I fancy, hover around pleasures that are purely mental, abandoning those in which the body is instrumental—provided that the man's love of wisdom is real, not artificial. . . . Such a person will be temperate and thoroughly uncovetous; for he is the last person in the world to value those objects, which make men anxious for money at any cost.

Plato, *The Republic*

You, Antipho, seem to think that happiness consists in luxury and extravagance; but I think that to want nothing is to resemble the gods, and that to want as little as possible is to make the nearest approach to the gods.

Xenophon, *The Memorabilia of Socrates*

Socrates was not only the most rigid of all men in the government of his passions and appetites, but also most able to withstand cold, heat, and every kind of labor; and, besides, so inured to frugality, that, though he possessed very little, he very easily made it a sufficiency.

Xenophon, *The Memorabilia of Socrates*

Without introducing the rewards and the reputation which justice confers, as you said that Homer and Hesiod do, have we not found that justice, taken by itself, is best for the soul, also taken by itself, and that the soul is bound to practice just actions, whether it possess the ring of Gyges, and, in addition to this ring, the helmet of Hades, or not? . . . Then may we now, Glaucon, proceed without offense to take into account those great and abundant rewards which justice, along with the rest of virtue, wins to the soul from gods and men, not only during a man's lifetime, but also after his death?

Plato, *The Republic*

For they do not know the penalty of wrongdoing which above all things they ought to know—not stripes and death as they suppose, which evildoers often escape, but a penalty which cannot be escaped. What is that? There are two patterns set before them, the one blessed and divine, the other godless and wretched, and they do not see in their utter folly and infatuation that they are growing like the one and unlike the other by reason of their evil deeds!

Plato, *Theætetus*

The soul of a philosopher will consider that it is the office of philosophy to set her free. . . . She gains for herself peace from worldly things, and follows reason and ever abides in it, contemplating what is true and divine and real, and fostered by them.

Plato, *Phædo*

A man should be of good cheer about his soul, if in his life he has renounced the pleasures and adornments of the body, because they were nothing to him, and because he thought that they would do him not good but harm; and if he has instead earnestly pursued the pleasures of learning, and adorned his soul with the adornment of temperance, and justice, and courage, and freedom, and truth, which belongs to her, and is her own, and so awaits his journey to the other world, in readiness to set forth whenever fate calls him.

Plato, *Phædo*

This . . . is . . . the moment approaching death when everything is at stake with a man; and for this reason, above all others, it is the duty of each of us diligently to investigate and study, to the neglect of every other subject, that system of thought which may happily enable a man to learn and discover who will render him so instructed, as to be able to discriminate between a good and an evil life, . . . giving the name of evil to the life which will draw the soul into becoming more unjust, and the name of good to the life which will lead it to become more just, and bidding farewell to every other consideration. For we have seen that in life and in death it is best to choose thus. With iron resolution must he hold fast this opinion when he enters the future world, in order that, there as well as here, he may escape being dazzled by wealth and similar evil and may not plunge into usurpations or other corresponding courses of action, to the inevitable detriment of others, and to his own still heavier affliction; but may know how to select that life which always steers a middle course between such extremes, and to shun excess on either side to the best of his power, not only in this life, but also in that which is to come. For, by acting thus, he is sure to become a most happy man.

Plato, *The Republic*

Indeed, my dear Glaucon, the choice between becoming a good or a bad man involves a great stake—yes, a greater stake than people suppose. Therefore it is wrong to be heedless of justice and the rest of virtue, under the excitement of honor, wealth, power or even poetry.

Plato, *The Republic*

My friend, if you think that a man of any worth at all ought to reckon the chances of life and death when he acts, or that he ought to think of anything but whether he is acting rightly or wrongly, and as a good or a bad man would act, you are grievously mistaken.... Wherever a man's post is, whether he has chosen it of his own will, or whether he has been placed at it by his commander, there it is his duty to remain and face the danger, without thinking of death, or of any other thing, except dishonor.

Plato, *The Apology*

When someone asked him what object of study he thought best for a man, he replied, "Good conduct."

Xenophon, *The Memorabilia of Socrates*

I imagine we shall assert that in fact poets and writers of prose are alike in error in the most important particulars, when they speak of men, making out that many are happy, though unjust, and many just, yet miserable, and that injustice is profitable if it be not found out, whereas justice is a gain to your neighbor, but a loss to yourself.

Plato, *The Republic*

Good language and good harmony and grace and good rhythm all depend upon a good nature, by which I do not mean that silliness which by courtesy we call good nature, but a mind that is really well and nobly constituted in its moral character. If so, then must not our young men on all occasions pursue these qualities, if we intend them to perform their proper work?

Plato, *The Republic*

I do not think it true to say that where there is fear, there is also reverence. Many people who fear sickness and poverty and other such evils, seem to me to have fear, but no reverence for what they fear. . . . But I think that where there is reverence, there is also fear. Does any man feel reverence and a sense of shame about anything, without at the same time dreading and fearing the character of baseness?

Plato, *Euthyphron*

And is it right to repay evil with evil, as the world thinks, or not right?

We ought not to repay wrong with wrong or do harm to any man, no matter what we may have suffered from him.

Plato, *Crito*

When Socrates maintained that to be busy was useful and beneficial for a man, and that to be unemployed was noxious and ill for him, that to work was a good, and to be idle an evil, he at the same time observed that those only who do something good, really work and are useful workmen, but those who gamble or do anything bad and pernicious, he called idle.

Xenophon, *The Memorabilia of Socrates*

Concerning what idleness was, he said that he found most men did something, for that dice-players and buffoons did something; but he said that all such persons were idle, for it was in their power to go and do something better.

Xenophon, *The Memorabilia of Socrates*

Socrates said, too, that justice, and every other virtue, was prudence, for that everything just, and everything done agreeably to virtue, was honorable and good; that those who could discern those things, would never prefer anything else to them; that those who could not discern them, would never be able to do them, but would even go wrong if they attempted to do them; and that the prudent, accordingly, did what was honorable and good, but that the imprudent could not do it, but went wrong even if they attempted to do it; and that since, therefore, all past actions, and all actions that are honorable and good, are done in agreement with virtue, it is manifest that justice and every other virtue is prudence.

Xenophon, *The Memorabilia of Socrates*

Can the man whose mind is well-regulated, and free from covetousness, meanness, pretentiousness, and cowardice, be by any possibility hard to deal with or unjust?

Plato, *The Republic*

Good men and bad men are very few indeed, and the majority of men are neither one nor the other.

Plato, *Phædo*

It is the property, not of the just man, but of his opposite, the unjust man, to hurt either friend or any other creature.

Plato, *The Republic*

In no instance, is it just to injure anybody.

Plato, *The Republic*

## 18

# Obedience to the Law

THE GREATEST BLESSING to states, moreover, is concord . . . without such unanimity, no state can be well governed, nor any family well regulated.

Xenophon, *The Memorabilia of Socrates*

Suppose the laws and the commonwealth were to come and appear to me as I was preparing to run away (if that is the right phrase to describe my escape) and were to ask: "Tell us, Socrates, what have you in your mind to do? What do you mean by trying to escape, but to destroy us the laws, and the whole city, so far as in you lies? Do you think that a state can exist and not be overthrown, in which the decisions of law are of no force, and are disregarded and set at naught by private individuals?" . . . Shall I reply: "But the state has injured me; it has decided my cause wrongly?"

Shall we say that? . . . And suppose the laws were to reply: "Was that our agreement? Or was it that you would submit to whatever judgments the state should pronounce? . . . Or, are you too wise to see that your country is worthier, and more august, and more sacred, and holier, and held in higher honor both by the gods and by all men of understanding, than your father and your mother and all your other ancestors, and that it is your bounden duty to reverence it, and to submit to it, and to approach it more humbly than you would approach your father, when it is angry with you; and either to do whatever it bids you to do or to persuade it to excuse you; and to obey in silence if it orders you to endure stripes or imprisonment, or if it send you to battle to be wounded or to die? That is what is your duty. You must not give way, nor retreat, nor desert your post. In war, and in the court of justice, and everywhere, you must do whatever your city and your country bid you do, or you must convince them that their commands are unjust."

Plato, *Crito*

Have you ever heard it said of Lycurgus, the Lacedæ-monian, . . . that he would not have made Sparta at all different from other states, if he had not established in it, beyond others, a spirit of obedience to the laws?

Xenophon, *The Memorabilia of Socrates*

The virtue of the state may . . . be chiefly traced to the presence of that fourth principle in every child and woman, in every slave, freeman, and artisan, in the ruler and in the subject, requiring each to do his own work, and not meddle with many things.

Plato, *The Republic*

# 19

# Honoring Parents

D**O YOU NOT** know that the state takes no account of any other species of ingratitude, nor allows any action at law for it, overlooking such as receive a favor and make no return for it; but that, if a person does not pay due regard to his parents, it imposes a punishment on him, rejects his services, and does not allow him to hold the archonship, considering that such a person cannot piously perform the sacrifices offered for the country, or discharge any other duty with propriety and justice? Indeed, if any one does not keep up the sepulchers of his dead parents, the state inquires into it in the examinations of candidates for office.

Xenophon, *The Memorabilia of Socrates*

Whom, then, can we find receiving greater benefits from any persons than children receive from their parents—children whom their parents have brought from non-existence into existence, to view so many beautiful objects, and to share in so many blessings, as the gods grant to men; blessings which appear to us so inestimable, that we shrink, in the highest degree, from relinquishing them; and governments have made death the penalty for the most heinous crimes, in the supposition that they could not suppress in justice by the terror of any greater evil?

Xenophon, *The Memorabilia of Socrates*

## 20

# Marriage and Family

THE JUST MAN ... is the last man in the world to be guilty of adultery.

Plato, *The Republic*

Does it not then, appear to you shameful for a man to yield to the same influence as the most senseless of animals, as adulterers, for instance, knowing that the adulterer is in danger of suffering what the law threatens and of being watched and disgraced if caught, yet enter into closets; and, though there are such dangers and dishonors hanging over the intriguer and so many occupations that will free him from the desire for sensual gratification, does it not seem to you the part of one tormented by an evil genius, to run nevertheless into imminent peril?

Xenophon, *The Memorabilia of Socrates*

Parents should not beget . . . children beyond their means, through a prudent fear of poverty.

Plato, *The Republic*

Aristarchus: "I have living with me free-born persons and relatives." . . .

"Then," said Socrates; "because they are free and related to you, do you think that they ought to do nothing else but eat and sleep? Among other free persons, do you see that those who live thus spend their time more pleasantly, and do you consider them happier, than those who practice the arts which they know, and which are useful to support life? Do you find that idleness and carelessness are serviceable to mankind, either for learning what it becomes them to know, or for remembering what they have learned, or for maintaining the health and strength of their bodies, or for acquiring and preserving what is useful for the support of life, and that industry and diligence are of no service at all? . . . Under present circumstances, as I should suppose, you neither feel attached to your relatives, nor they to you, for you find them burdensome to you, and they see that you are annoyed with their company. With such feelings there is danger that dislike may grow stronger and stronger, and that previous friendly inclination may be diminished. But if you take them under your direction, so that they may be employed, you will love them, when you see that they are serviceable to you, and they will grow attached to you, when they find that you feel satisfaction in their society; and, remembering past services with greater pleasure, you will increase the friendly feeling resulting from them, and consequently grow more attached and better disposed toward each other."

Xenophon, *The Memorabilia of Socrates*

You do not surely suppose that men beget children merely to gratify their passions, since the streets are full, as well as the brothels, of means to allay desire; but what we evidently consider is, from what sort of women the finest children may be born to us and, uniting with them, we beget children.

Xenophon, *The Memorabilia of Socrates*

## 21

# Rights of Women

Say leading women, too, Glaucon; for do not suppose that my remarks were intended to apply at all more to men than to women, so long as we can find women whose talents are equal to the situation.

Plato, *The Republic*

If the question is how to render a woman fit for the office of guardian, we shall not have one education for men, and another for women, especially as the nature to be wrought upon is the same in both cases.

Plato, *The Republic*

None of the occupations which comprehend the ordering of a state belong to woman as woman, nor yet to man as man; but natural gifts are to be found here and there, in both sexes alike; and, so far as her nature is concerned, the woman is admissible to all pursuits as well as the man; though in all of them the woman is weaker than the man.

Plato, *The Republic*

We shall hold, I imagine, that one woman may have talents for medicine, and another be without them; and that one may be musical, and another unmusical. . . . And shall we not also say, that one woman may have qualifications for gymnastic exercises, and for war, and another be unwarlike, and without a taste for gymnastics? . . . Again, may there not be a love of knowledge in one and distaste for it in another? And may not one be spirited, and another spiritless? . . . If that be so, there are some women who are fit, and others who are unfit, for the office of guardian. For were not those the qualities that we selected, in the case of the men, as marking their fitness for that office? . . . Then as far as the guardianship of a state is concerned, there is no difference between the natures of the man and of the woman, but only various degrees of weakness and strength. . . . Then we shall have to select duly qualified women also, to share in the life and official labors of the duly qualified men; since we find that they are competent to the work, and of kindred nature with the man.

Plato, *The Republic*

# 22

# Friendship

66 Is it not everywhere a law, also," said Socrates, "that men should do good to those who do good to them?" "It is a law," answered Hippias, "but it is transgressed." "Do not those therefore who transgress it incur punishment," continued Socrates, "by being deprived of good friends, and being compelled to have recourse to those who hate them?"

Xenophon, *The Memorabilia of Socrates*

If you enable me also to say concerning you, that you are attentive to your friends, that you delight in nothing so much as in the possession of good friends, that you pride yourself on the honorable conduct of your friends not less than at your own, that you rejoice at the good fortune of your friends not less than at your own, that you are never weary of contriving means by which good fortune may come to your friends and that you think it the great virtue of a man to surpass his friends in doing them good and his enemies in doing them harm, I think that I shall be a very useful assistant to you in gaining the affections of worthy friends.

Xenophon, *The Memorabilia of Socrates*

Considering what envy was, he decided it to be a certain uneasiness, not such as arises, however, at the failure of friends, nor such as is felt at the good success of enemies, but those only, he said, were envious who were annoyed at the good success of their friends.

Xenophon, *The Memorabilia of Socrates*

Friendship insinuating itself through all the hindrances unites together the honorable and good; for such characters, through affection for virtue, prefer the enjoyment of a moderate competency without strife, to the attainment of unlimited power by means of war; they can endure hunger and thirst without discontent, and take only a fair share of meat and drink, and, though delighted with the attractions of youthful beauty, they can control themselves, so as to forbear from offending those whom they ought not to offend.... By laying aside all avaricious feelings too, they can not only be satisfied with their lawful share of the common property, but can even assist one another. They can settle their differences, not only without mutual offence, but even to their mutual benefit. They can prevent their anger from going so far as to cause them repentance; and envy they entirely banish, by sharing their own property with their friends, and considering that of their friends as their own.

Xenophon, *The Memorabilia of Socrates*

It would be well for each of us to examine himself to consider of what value he is in the estimation of his friends; and to try to be of as much value to them as possible, in order that his friends may be less likely to desert him; for I often hear one man saying that his friend has abandoned him and another, that a person whom he thought to be his friend has preferred a mina to him.

Xenophon, *The Memorabilia of Socrates*

But strive with good courage, Critobulus, to be good yourself, and, having become so, endeavor to gain the friendship of men of honor and virtue. Perhaps I myself also may be able to assist you in this pursuit of the honorable and virtuous, from being naturally disposed to love; since, for whatever persons I conceive a liking, I devote myself with ardor, and with my whole mind, to love them, and be loved in return by them, regretting their absence to have mine regretted by them, and longing for their society while they on the other hand long for mine.

Xenophon, *The Memorabilia of Socrates*

Tell me, Chærecrates, you surely are not one of those men, are you, who think wealth more valuable than brothers, when wealth is but a senseless thing and a brother endowed with reason; when wealth needs protection, while a brother can afford protection; and when wealth, besides, is plentiful, and a brother but one?

Xenophon, *The Memorabilia of Socrates*

"And do you advise me, too," said Thedota, later mistress of Alcibiades, "to weave a net?" "Yes," said Socrates, "for you ought not to think that you will catch friends, the most valuable prey that can be taken, without art. Do you not see how many arts hunters use to catch hares, an animal of but little worth?" . . .

"By what art of this kind, then," said she, "can I catch friends?" "If," said he, "instead of a dog, you got somebody to track and discover the lovers of beauty, and the wealthy, and who, when he has found them, will contrive to drive them into your nets." "And what nets have I?" said she.

"You have one at least," he replied, "and one that closely embraces its prey, your person; and in it you have a mind, by which you understand how you may gratify a person by looking at him, and what you may say to cheer him, and learn that you ought to receive with transport him who shows concern for you, and to shut out him who is insolent, to attend carefully on a friend when he is ill, to rejoice greatly with him when he has succeeded in anything honorable, and to cherish affection in your whole soul for the man who sincerely cares for you."

Xenophon, *The Memorabilia of Socrates*

"Tell me, Critobolus," said Socrates, "If we were in need of a good friend, how should we proceed to look for one? Should we not, in the first place, seek for a person who can govern his appetite, his inclination to wine or sensuality, and abstain from immoderate sleep and idleness?"

Xenophon, *The Memorabilia of Socrates*

# 23

# Training

THOSE WHO THOUGHT that they had good natural abilities, but despised instruction, he endeavored to convince that minds which show most natural power have most need of education, pointing out to them that horses of the best breed, which are high-spirited and stubborn, become, if they are broken when young, most useful and valuable, but if they are left unbroken, remain quite unmanageable and worthless; and that hounds of the best blood, able to endure toil and eager to attack beasts, prove, if they are well trained, most serviceable for the chase, and every way excellent, but, if untrained, are useless, rabid, and unruly. . . . In like manner he showed that men of the best natural endowments, possessed of the greatest strength of mind, and most energetic in executing what they undertake, become, if well-disciplined and instructed in what they ought to do, most estimable characters, and most beneficent to society (as they then performed most numerous and important services), but that, if uninstructed, and left in ignorance, they proved utterly worthless and mischievous; for that, not knowing what line of conduct they ought to pursue, they often entered upon evil courses and, being haughty and impetuous, were difficult to be restrained or turned from their purpose, and thus occasioned very many and great evils. . . . But those who prided themselves on their wealth, and thought that they required no education, but imagined that their riches would suffice to effect whatever they desired, and to gain them honor from mankind, he tried to reduce to reason by saying that the man was a fool who thought that he could distinguish the good and the evil in life without instruction and that he also was a fool who, though he could not distinguish them, thought that he would procure whatever he wished and effect whatever was for his interest, by means of his wealth.

Xenophon, *The Memorabilia of Socrates*

His virtue is not free from blemish owing to his having parted from the best guardian, . . . rational inquiry, . . . blended with music; for this alone by its presence and indwelling can preserve its owner in the possession of lifelong virtue.

Plato, *The Republic*

A child cannot discriminate between what is allegory and what is not; and whatever at that age is adopted as a matter of belief, has a tendency to become fixed and indelible; and therefore, perhaps, we ought to esteem it of the greatest importance that the fictions which children first hear should be adapted in the most perfect manner to the promotion of virtue.

Plato, *The Republic*

Arithmetic, therefore, and geometry, and all the branches of that preliminary education which is to pave the way for dialectic, must be taught our pupils in their childhood—care being taken to convey instruction in such a shape as not to make it compulsory upon them to learn. This is . . . because . . . no trace of slavery ought to mix with the studies of the freeborn man. For the constrained performance of bodily labors does, it is true, exert no evil influence upon the body; but in the case of the mind, no study, pursued under compulsion, remains rooted in the memory.

. . . Hence, my excellent friend, you must train the children to their studies in a playful manner, and without any air of constraint, with the further object of discerning more readily the natural bent of their respective characters.

Plato, *The Republic*

Of all men that I have known, he was the most anxious to discover in what occupation each of those who attended to him was likely to prove skillful; and of all that it becomes a man of honor and virtue to know, he taught them himself whatever he knew, with the utmost cheerfulness; and what he had not sufficient knowledge to teach, he took them to those who knew, to learn.

Xenophon, *The Memorabilia of Socrates*

But the shortest, and safest, and best way, Critobulus, is to strive to be really good in that in which you wish to be thought good. Whatever are called virtues among mankind, you will find, on consideration, capable of being increased by study and exercise.

Xenophon, *The Memorabilia of Socrates*

Virtue is not a thing that can be taught.

Plato, *Protagoras*

Does it not follow, from our previous admission, that any individual may pursue with success one calling, but not many; or, if he attempts this, by his meddling with many he will fail in all, so far as to gain no distinction in any?

Plato, *The Republic*

Ought we not . . . to seek out artists . . . who by the power of genius can trace out the nature of the fair and the graceful, that our young men, dwelling as it were in a healthful region, may drink in good from every quarter, whence any emanation from noble works may strike upon their eye or their ear, like a gale wafting health from salubrious lands, and win them imperceptibly from their earliest childhood into resemblance, love, and harmony with the true beauty of reason?

Plato, *The Republic*

When is a man likely to succeed best? When he divides his exertions among many trades, or when he devotes himself exclusively to one?

Plato, *The Republic*

No two persons are born exactly alike, but each differs from each in natural endowments, one being suited for one occupation, and another for another.

Plato, *The Republic*

In youth and boyhood they ought to be put through a course of training in philosophy, suited to their years.

Plato, *The Republic*

Later when their bodily powers begin to fail, and they are released from public duties and military service, from that time forward they ought to lead a dedicated life and consecrate themselves to this one pursuit (i.e. philosophy), if they are to live happily on earth, and

after death to crown the life they have led with a corresponding destiny in another world.

Plato, *The Republic*

## 24

# Care of the Body

H<small>E EARNESTLY RECOMMENDED</small> those who conversed with him to take care of their health, both by learning whatever they could respecting it from men of experience, and by attending to it, each for himself, throughout his whole life, studying what food or drink, or what exercise, was most suitable for him, and how he might act in regard to them so as to enjoy the best health; for he said it would be difficult for a person who thus attended to himself to find a physician that would tell better than himself what was conducive to his health.

Xenophon, *The Memorabilia of Socrates*

Do you not know that those who are by nature the weakest, become, by exercising their bodies, stronger in those things in which they exercise them, than those who neglect them, and bear the fatigue of exercise with greater ease? And do you not think that I, who am constantly preparing my body by exercise to endure whatever may happen to it, bear everything more easily than you who take no exercise?

Xenophon, *The Memorabilia of Socrates*

It is not proper to attempt to cure the eyes without the head, nor the head without the body; so neither is it proper to cure the body without the soul. . . . When this is not in a good state, it is impossible for a part to be well.

Plato, *Charmides*

He did not approve that a person should eat to excess, and then use immoderate exercise, but recommended that he should work off, by a proper degree of exercise, as much as the appetite received with pleasure.

Xenophon, *The Memorabilia of Socrates*

Another person saying that he ate without pleasure, "Acumenus," said Socrates, "prescribes an excellent remedy for that disease." The other asking, "What sort of remedy?" "To abstain from eating," said Socrates; "for he says that, after abstaining, you will live with more pleasure, less expense, and better health."

Xenophon, *The Memorabilia of Socrates*

In the dangers of war, not a few, through weakness of body, either lose their lives, or save them with dishonor; many, from the same causes, are taken alive and, as prisoners of war, endure for the rest of their lives, if such should be their fate, the bitterest slavery; or, falling into the most grievous hardships, and paying for their ransom sometimes more than they possess, pass the remainder of their existence in want of necessaries, and in the endurance of affliction; and many, too, incur infamy, being thought to be cowards merely from the imbecility of their bodily frame. . . . Yet the lot which falls to those who have their bodies in good condition is exactly the reverse of that which falls to those who have them in ill condition; for those who have their bodies in a good state are healthy and strong; and many, from being possessed of this advantage, save themselves with honor amid the struggles of war, and escape every peril; many, also, assist their friends and benefit their country, and, for such services, are thought worthy of favor, acquire great glory, and attain the highest dignities; and, on these accounts, pass the rest of their lives with greater pleasure and honor, and bequeath finer fortunes to their children. . . . Nor, because the city does not require warlike exercises publicly, ought we, on that account, to neglect them privately, but rather, to practice them the more; for be well assured that neither in any other contest, nor in any affair whatever, will you at all come off the worse because your body is better trained than those of other men, since the body must bear its part in whatever men do and in all the services required from the body, it is of the utmost importance to have it in the best possible condition. . . . For even in that in which you think that there is least exercise for the body, namely, thinking, who does not know that many fail greatly from ill-health? And loss of memory, despondency, irritability, and madness, often, from ill-health of body, attack the mind with such force as to drive out all previous knowledge.

Xenophon, *The Memorabilia of Socrates*

We certainly said, did we not, that our pupils must be trained in their youth to war?

Plato, *The Republic*

In pronouncing a city to be cowardly or brave, who would look to any but the portion of it which fights in its defense and takes the field in its behalf?

Plato, *The Republic*

# 25

# Death

THE PROPHETIC SIGN, which I am wont to receive from the divine voice, has been constantly with me all through my life till now, opposing me in quite small matters if I were not going to act rightly. And now you yourselves see what has happened to me, a thing which might be thought, and which is sometimes actually reckoned, the supreme evil. But the sign of God did not withstand me when I was leaving my house in the morning, nor when I was coming up hither to the court, nor at any point in my speech, when I was going to say anything, though at other times it has often stopped me in the very act of speaking. But now, in this matter, it has never once withstood me, either in my works or my actions. I will tell you what I believe to be the reason of that. This thing that has come upon me must be a good and those of us who think that death is an evil, must needs be mistaken. I have a clear proof that that is so; for my accustomed sign would certainly have opposed me, if I had not been going to fare well.

Plato, *The Apology*

To fear death, my friends, is only to think ourselves wise, without being wise; for it is to think that we know what we do not know. For everything that men can tell, death may be the greatest good that can happen to them; but they fear it as if they knew quite well that it was the greatest of evils. And what is this but that shameful ignorance of thinking that we know what we do not know?

Plato, *The Apology*

He who is truly a man, ought not to care about living a certain time; . . . he leaves all that to God and considers in what way he can spend his appointed term.

Plato, *Gorgias*

I have often seen men with a reputation behaving in a strange way at their trial, as if they thought it a terrible fate to be killed, and as though they expected to live forever, if you did not put them to death.

Plato, *The Apology*

Does not the purification consist, as we have said, in separating the soul from the body, as far as is possible, and in accustoming her to collect and rally herself together from the body on every side, and to dwell alone by herself as much as she can, both now and hereafter, released from the bondage of the body?

Plato, *Phædo*

The true philosopher, we hold, is alone in his constant desire to set his soul from the body, is he not?... Would it not be absurd then, as I began by saying, for a man to complain at death coming to him.

Plato, *Phædo*

Like children, you are afraid that the wind will really blow the soul away and disperse her when she leaves the body, especially if a man happens to die in a storm and not in a calm.

Plato, *Phædo*

No bird sings when it is hungry, or cold, or in any pain; not even the nightingale, nor the swallow, nor the hoopoe, which, they assert, wail and sing for grief. But I think that neither these birds nor the swans sing for grief. I believe that the swans have prophetic power and foreknowledge of the good things in the next world, for they are Apollo's birds; and so they sing and rejoice on the day of their death, more than in all their life. And I believe that I myself am a fellow slave with the swans, and consecrated to the service of the same God, and that I have prophetic power from my master no less than they; and that I am not more despondent than they are at leaving this life.

Plato, Phædo

Do you think a man can ever become brave who is haunted by the fear of death? . . . Do you imagine that a believer in Hades and its terrors will be free from all fear of death, and in the day of battle will prefer it to defeat and slavery?

Plato, The Republic

But I do think, Cebes, that it is true that the gods are our guardians, and that we men are a part of their property. Do you not think so? . . . Well, then, . . . if one of your possessions were to kill itself, though you had not signified that you wished it to die, should you not be angry with it? Should you not punish it, if punishment were possible? . . . Then in this way perhaps it is not unreasonable to hold that no man has a right to take his own life, but that he must wait until God sends some necessity upon him, as has now been sent upon me.

Plato, Phædo

You have not gained very much time, Athenians, and, as the price of it, you will have an evil name from all who wish to revile the city, and they will cast in your teeth that you put Socrates, a wise man, to death. . . . But when I was defending myself, I thought that I ought not to do anything unmanly because of the danger which I ran, and I have not changed my mind now. I would very much rather defend myself as I did, and die, than as you would have had me do flee, and live. . . . I think that it is a much harder thing to escape from wickedness than from death; for wickedness is swifter than death.

Plato, The Apology

If I shall live a longer period, perhaps I shall be destined to sustain the evils of old age, to find my sight and hearing weakened, to feel my intellect impaired, to become less apt to learn, and more forgetful, and, in fine, to grow inferior to others in all those qualities in which I was once superior to them. If I should be insensible to this deterioration, life would not be worth retaining; and, if I should feel it, how could I live otherwise than with less profit, and with less comfort? If I am to die unjustly, my death will be a disgrace to those who unjustly kill me; for if injustice is a disgrace, must it not be a disgrace to do anything unjustly? But what disgrace will it be to me, that others could not decide, or act, justly with regard to me? Of the men who have lived before me, I see that the estimation left among posterity with regard to such as have, done wrong, and such as have suffered wrong, is by no means similar; and I know that I also, if now I die, shall obtain from mankind far different consideration from that which they will pay to those who take my life; for I know that they will always bear witness to me that I have never wronged any man, or rendered any man less virtuous, but that I have always endeavored to make those better who conversed with me.

Xenophon, *The Memorabilia of Socrates*

Do you think that a spirit full of lofty thoughts, and privileged to contemplate all time, and all existence, can possibly attach any great importance to this life? No, it is impossible. Then such a person will not regard death as a formidable thing, will he?

Plato, *The Republic*

# Bibliography

Dawson, Miles Menander, *The Ethics of Socrates*. New York: G. P. Putnam's Sons, 1924.

Plato, *Crito*, *Phædo*, *The Apology*, *Philebus*, *Euthyphron*. Translated by F. J. Church. M. A. London: MacMillan and Co., 1891.

——. *Gorgias*. Translated by Benjamin Jowett. New York: C. Scribner's Sons, 1871.

——. *Phædrus*, *Protagoras*, *Charmides*. Translated by J. Wright. London: MacMillan and Co., 1988.

——. *The Republic*. Translated by J. L. Davies and D. J. Vaughan. London: MacMillan and Co., 1866.

——. *Theætetus*. Translated by Benjamin Jowett. New York: C. Scribner's Sons, 1871.

Xenophon, *The Memorabilia of Socrates*. Translated by J. S. Watson. Philadelphia: David McKay Publishers, 1899.

# Index

## A

Acumenus 9, 102
adultery 83
Anaxagoras
    on fire and the sun 31–32
Antipho 68
Anytus 37
*Apology, The* 2, 5, 6, 10, 13,
        14, 15, 22, 23, 37, 39,
        43, 71, 106, 109, 111
appetites 67, 68
    three 60–61
Aristarchus 84

## B

beautiful persons 58
beauty 67, 90, 92, 99
    happiness and 20
    pleasure and 61
    the soul and 47–48

body, the
    and the soul 6–7, 41,
        47–54, 107
    care of 101–104
    exercise of 25
    health of 7, 9, 39, 57, 84,
        101–104
    labor and 97
    modesty and 65
    pleasure and 56, 67–68,
        69

## C

calling
    devotion to one 98
Cebes 50, 51, 108
Chærecrates 92
Chærephon 21–22
*Charmides* 21, 47, 102, 111
children 103, 107

begetting of 82, 84, 85
  training of 97
courage 39, 61, 70, 91
covetousness 74
cowardice 40, 74
Critias 58
Critobulus 91, 98
*Crito* 10, 43, 67, 73, 78, 111

**D**

death
  as God's choice 106
  compared to life 110
  duty and 71
  existence after 50, 100, 107–108
  fear of 10–11, 106, 108
  moment approaching 70
  self-inflicted 108
  wrongdoing and 51, 69, 82, 106, 109
Delphi 21, 35
desire
  freedom from 8
  influence on the mind 33

**E**

eating 8, 9, 50, 58
  abstaining from 102
  appetite and 59

education 52, 87, 95–97
  nature of 19–20
emotions
  as rulers vs. subjects of the mind 34
endowments, natural 95, 99
envy 90, 91
Euthydemus 20, 35, 42, 58
*Euthyphron* 73, 111
evil 6, 23, 65, 82, 97
  and the moment approaching death 70–71
  death as 105, 106, 108
  idleness as 73
  in marriage 83
  instruction and 96
  oratory 29
  penalties of 69
  pleasure and 64
  reason and 26
  repaying evil with 73
  self-knowledge and 36
  souls reincarnated in animals 53
  the soul and 49, 52–53
evils 10, 35, 51, 72, 96, 106, 109
exercise
  bodily health and 7, 25, 26, 98, 101–102, 104

## F

fear
  and reverence 72–73
friends and friendship 8,
    89–93, 103
  attentiveness to 89–90
  envy at good success of 90
  how to catch 92–93
  insinuating itself
      through all hin-
      drances 90–91
  nurturing value to 91
  with the good and
      honorable 91

## G

Glaucon 69, 71, 87
God (gods) 31, 45–46, 69,
    78, 82
  complete knowledge of
      45–46
  good things and 45
  men as property of 108
  provisions of 42
  resemblance to 68
  reverence for 45
  the soul and 50–51
  wisdom of 13
good nature 72
good, the 17–20, 47, 89
  ability to discern 96

as highest object of
    thought 17–18
pleasure and 56
the afterlife and 50, 107
*Gorgias* 10, 106, 111

## H

happiness 20, 51, 68, 71, 72
health. *See* body, the;
    health of
Hippias 89

## I

idleness 84, 93
  definition of 73
injustice 53, 109
  as profitable 66, 72

## J

judgmentalism 23
justice
  as a loss to yourself 72
  as prudent 74
  the soul and 68–69, 70
  the unrighteous and 33
  virtue and 39, 71

## K

knowledge 7, 15, 17, 19, 22,
    53, 61, 88
  of self 21, 36

# L

law
  obedience to 77–79
life, unexamined 37
living well 67
logic 30
  central role of 3, 18
love
  artistic imitation of 34,
    99
  beautiful persons and 58
  falling in 59
  friendship and 91
  legitimate 60
Lycurgus 78

# M

meanness 74
*Memorabilia of Socrates,
  The* 7, 8, 9, 20, 25,
    32, 36, 40, 42, 45,
    46, 48, 57, 58, 59, 63,
    64, 68, 72, 73, 74,
    77, 78, 81, 82, 83, 85,
    89, 90, 91, 92, 93,
    96, 98, 101, 102, 104,
    110, 111
middle course 71
mind, the
  exercise of 25, 97
money 6, 8, 38, 57, 61, 68

# O

observation 31–32
occupation 98–99
old age 109

# P

parents, honoring 81–82
*Phædo* 4, 5, 6, 7, 9, 15, 26,
    29, 39, 40, 49, 50, 51,
    52, 53, 54, 55, 58, 69,
    70, 74, 107, 108, 111
*Phædrus* 29, 40, 48, 67, 111
*Philebus* 5, 19, 27, 41, 42,
    55, 56, 111
philosopher
  soul of 9, 69
  true 107
Plato 1–3
pleasure 19, 34, 40, 51,
    55–62, 85, 103
  and the acquisition of
    money 8
  beautiful persons and 58
  best and most appropri-
    ate 60
  eating or drinking and
    8–9, 59, 102
  enslavement to 64
  false 56
  love and 60
  of health 57

of learning 69–70
pain and 55–57
the unwise and 66–67
virtue and 39
power 71, 90
pretentiousness 74
*Protagoras* 48, 67, 98, 111
prudence
as every other virtue 74

R

reality 18, 41–42
reason 19, 25–27, 92, 96, 99
as sovereign principle 25
in the pursuit of reality 3–4, 18
pleasure and 60
the philosopher and 9, 69
the soul and 6, 52
vs. the emotions 34
vs. the senses 5, 18, 26
relatives
when burdensome 84
*Republic, The* 2, 4, 11, 15, 17, 18, 19, 20, 25, 26, 27, 30, 33, 34, 40, 41, 46, 47, 48, 49, 54, 57, 60, 62, 65, 66, 67, 68, 69, 71, 72, 74, 75, 79, 83, 84, 87, 88, 96,

97, 98, 99, 100, 104, 108, 110, 111
reverence
fear and 72–73

S

self, the, knowledge of 21, 36
Simmias 50
Socrates. *See also* Socratic Method
commitment to health 7, 101–102
death of 2, 109
frugality of 9, 57
self-discipline of 68
service to God 5, 13, 37, 38, 40
Socratic Method 1–2, 13–14
sophistry 29–30
soul, the 47–54
divine nature of 49
evil and 29, 49, 52–53, 70
immortal nature of 52
justice and 68–69
learning faculty residing in 19
perfection of 38
pleasure and 56
the body and 6, 48–54, 107
wrong use of words and 29

swans
    knowledge of afterlife
        107–108

# T

temperance 39, 63–64, 70
    intemperance 64
*Theætetus* 4, 20, 46, 69,
        111
Thedota 92
truth 6, 15–16, 19, 30, 38,
        39, 47, 52, 57, 60, 61,
        62, 70
    as distinct from good 17

# V

vanity 5
vengeance 10
virtue 14, 38, 66
    and the unexamined
        life 37
    as the plumage of the
        soul 67
    friendship and 90–91
    prudence and 74
    purifying aspect of 39
    rewards of 69
    temperance as the foun-
        dation of 64
    training of 96–98
    wrong to be heedless
        of 71

# W

war 78, 88, 90, 103, 104
wealth 20, 70, 71, 92, 96
    from virtue 39
wisdom
    gained after death 52–53
    love of 40, 51, 60–62,
        68
    modesty about 21–22
    of God vs. men 13
    of Socrates and Plato 3
    pleasure and 60
    the soul and 6, 38, 51
    the unwise and 66–67
    virtue and 39, 67
women
    office of guardian and
        87–88
    when equal to men 87
wrongdoing
    unseen penalty of 69

# X

Xenophon 1, 7, 8, 9, 20, 25,
        32, 36, 40, 42, 45,
        46, 48, 57, 58, 59, 63,
        64, 68, 72, 73, 74,
        77, 78, 81, 82, 83, 85,
        89, 90, 91, 92, 93,
        96, 98, 101, 102, 104,
        110, 111